D0125758

TABLE OF CONTENTS

Acknowledgments

This book is made possible by many people's contributions. Special thanks to Mariko Yamasaki of the U.S. Forest Service, Steve Spencer of Maine's Bureau of Public Lands, Sylvia Plumb of Vermont's Green Mountain Club, Warren Hill (the "Voice of the Mountains" on the White Mountain National Forest radio station), John Bernardin, proprietor of the Notchland Inn, publishing consultant Jeannette Hopkins, and last, but by no means least, my wife, Roon, for her constructive criticism and constant support.

Introduction

Discovering Nature in New England's Mountains is an informal overview written for those who want to know something about nature in the mountains - but not too much. I have made every effort to keep this book simple. Overly-detailed technical explanations not only would have made this book three times as thick, but also would have defeated the purpose of writing it in the first place.

I make no claims to being a professional naturalist, but am instead a writer with a love of nature. My job here is to gather the most interesting and relevant information about nature in the mountains and present it simply. If, after reading this book, you want to learn more about something you read here, I will have done my job. Many publications and educational programs are available for serious investigation.

To get the most out of *Discovering Nature in New England's Mountains,* read it before you start your explorations. Then carry it with you as you venture into the woods, using it for reference.

We will look at things from a distance first, and then more closely, going from lower to upper elevations. Each view is different and fascinating in its own way.

Composite illustrations precede Chapters 2-5 showing most of the plants and animals described in the text. Enlarged details from these illustrations accompany most species descriptions. Please understand that to keep things simple we have taken some license with the illustrations. Don't expect to see all the species depicted at the same time or in the same context. After reading about the plants and animals that interest you, try to find them in the composite illustration. Then the fun begins: trying to find them in real life.

Not every living thing is described here - only what you are likely to see - but you must keep your eyes and ears open. Once you do that, whether you are back-packing for a week or simply escaping for a short day trip, these mountains will come to life.

And please do your share to help preserve this fragile environment by remembering the motto: "Take nothing but pictures; leave nothing but tracks."

Chapter 1
The Shape of the Land

Most visitors to northern New England love the scenery because, while it offers breathtaking vistas, it doesn't overwhelm you. From a distance, the mountains appear rounded and gentle. But as you look more closely, you will see rough shapes and patterns in the landscape that indicate a less than tranquil past.

Over millions of years, these mountains have undergone massive transformations. In prehistoric times, perhaps 350 million years ago, all of New England was covered by a warm, shallow sea; more recently, the land rose, forming sharp, craggy peaks, only to be eroded by millions of years of wind and rain. The most recent great event to shape the landscape occurred when a huge, mile-thick blanket of ice covered most of the region. It lasted from 3 million to 10,000 years ago.

Creeping only a few inches a day, the ice sheet scoured the ridges and rounded the peaks, transporting most of the topsoil to sea. It widened the valleys, shaping them into smooth, concave-sided troughs. When the ice melted, it left the landscape littered with rocks and boulders. Sometimes the ice sheet tore large boulders from their source rocks, dragging them

The "Mount Ascutney Train is a line of boulders taken from their source rocks during the last glacier. It stretches from Mount Ascutney, near Windsor, Vermont, all the way into Massachusetts.

great distances. You can see such "erratics" perched on the shoulders of mountains and even in the woods of the

valleys below.

Around Mount Washington, in New Hampshire, you
can see cirques from the road. These steep, smooth-sided
half-bowls were scalloped by glaciers during the Ice Age.
Ten of these "gulfs" or "ravines" can be found in the
Presidential Range. In Maine, glacial cirques can be seen
on Crocker Mountain (near Sugarloaf), Goose-eye Mountain in the Mahoosucs, and around Mount Katahdin
where they are known locally as "basins." The Mount
Mansfield area of Vermont also has cirques.

Many ponds in northern New England were created
by large blocks of ice melting in depressions of glacial
debris. These are called kettle ponds. Because there are
no outlets, the water doesn't circulate, and many ponds
have turned into cold, stagnant bogs with their own self-
sustaining communities of strange plants, including some
that eat insects.

The Sky

More than half the year the peaks of northern New
England are shrouded in clouds. This is another way of
saying that they are fog-bound, for fog is nothing more
than a cloud that is touching the ground. Frequently in
winter, fog at high elevations freezes, turning into rime,
coating everything with white frost.

Mountains act as barriers to air masses, causing them
to rise and cool; the moisture in the air condenses, forming clouds that often produce rain or snow. The peaks
can have twice as much rainfall as lower elevations.

These mountains are also cold. If you were to travel due east from northern New England, you would reach the palm-studded French Riviera, but it is no warmer here than Anchorage, Alaska. This is because most weather systems converge on New England, with circulations that pull cold winds down from Canada. As you will see, all this rain, wind, and cold affects everything that grows here.

Distant Patterns

On the slopes, look for thin lines of light green etched into the darker green stands of coniferous trees. These pale markings are usually abandoned logging roads, now taken over by Yellow Birches. Lumbermen used skids to drag logs through the forest, tearing up the ground in the process. Yellow Birches take advantage of these disruptions, as they thrive in sunlight and produce large quantities of light-weight seeds that rapidly spread throughout the forest. While Yellow Birches grow quickly, they won't last, for they have difficulty reproducing in their own shade. One day they will be replaced by shade-loving spruces, and the line of light green leaves will disappear.

In all of nature nothing remains the same. Whole forests change in a process called succession, where one plant or animal takes the place of another as conditions change.

Throughout the world, aging forests rejuvenate themselves. Insect infestations usually help the process. But in New England's mountains the weather is too cold for serious insect damage. Forests here have their own

unique way of rejuvenation. Look at wind-exposed hill-
sides for silvery bands of dying trees, perhaps 200 feet
apart. These are known as "fir waves."

Fir waves occur when all the trees in an area start out
as saplings at the same time, often after a forest fire. The
young trees grow up so quickly that before long they
compete for the same space. Eventually they can no
longer maintain themselves and lose their foliage.

As the trees die and topple over, an opening is created
for new trees to grow. The first trees to fall are those most
exposed to the wind. The space opened up is soon occu-
pied by saplings. But now the second row of trees is
exposed to the wind and blows over, creating another
space for newer saplings, and so on.

Over ten years or so, the landscape is covered again
with fir trees - only this time, they are of different ages.
The oldest and tallest are in a line in the front, where the
first trees had originally blown down. Successive younger
and shorter trees grow in lines behind each other, creating a wave effect.

Another distant pattern in the landscape is a pure
stand of Paper Birches. These beautiful, white-barked
trees proliferate after fires, as they grow quickly in openings exposed to sunlight - another way that forests rejuvenate themselves.

Paper Birches also outline avalanche tracks. Look for
them in ravines and gulches, especially around Mounts
Washington and Katahdin.

Yet another pattern to look for in the mountains is a
field of broken rocks. In cold weather, water that has
seeped into cracks in the bedrock expands as it turns into

ice, shattering large formations into smaller rocks. This leads to the creation of large areas covered with jagged blocks. The German word for this phenomenon is _felsenmeer_, or "sea of rocks."

Chapter 2
Nature at the Lower Elevations:
The Northern Hardwoods Zone

In the mountains the landscape changes with elevation because the soils and weather also change. At the
lower elevations, extending up to
about 3,000 feet, you will find a
community of trees, plants, birds,
and animals known as the Northern
Hardwoods Zone. Since most trails
begin below 3,000 feet, almost all
hikers will pass through this zone
first. (For example, both Pinkham
Notch in the White Mountains of
New Hampshire and Smuggler's
Notch in the Green Mountains of
Vermont are at about 2,000 feet;
Grafton Notch in the Mahoosuc Range of Maine is at
1,000 feet.)

*Climbing 400 feet up
a mountain is equiva-
lent to traveling about
100 miles further
north. The average
temperature drops
approximately five
degrees for each 1,000
feet of elevation.
Almost twice as much
precipitation falls on
the summits as falls in
the valleys.*

At the end of the Ice Age, rain and melting snow
carried rocky glacial debris down the mountain slopes,
forming deeper and better drained soils at lower elevations. These soils contained enough nutrients for hardwoods to take root. A few species of hardwoods that
could tolerate the cold began to dominate the valleys,
pushing hardy spruces and firs higher up the slopes
where it was colder, wetter, and windier.

You will most likely start hiking in a forest of mature
hardwoods with a floor that is lumpy and irregular from

decomposing stumps and logs. The ground is littered with leaves and needles. Trees here have large trunks and are spaced widely apart. Their tops will have intercepted most of the sunlight, so you will be in the shade most of the time. Occasionally you will come to openings created by trees blown down by the wind; these gaps usually contain a diversity of plants that can only thrive in sunlight.

TALL TREES (The Canopy)

The most common large trees to look for in the Northern Hardwoods Zone are Sugar Maple, American Beech, and Yellow Birch. You will also find two evergreens in abundance: Eastern Hemlock and White Pine.

Sugar Maple

Sugar maples are best known for spectacular red and yellow leaves in the fall. And, of course, maple syrup, a delicacy that Native Americans taught the pioneers to make. In the spring, 200-250 gallons of sap rise through a mature tree every day. Each sugar maple can produce anywhere from five to sixty gallons of sap per year. To make maple syrup you must tap the sap from the trunk and boil it down. It takes 32 gallons of sap to make one gallon of syrup.

Identification: Look for opposite leaves with five pointed lobes and U-shaped spaces between the lobes. The leaves are usually wider than they are long. Twigs are glossy, reddish. Branches start high up.

American Beech

These are sometimes called "bear trees," as bears love beechnuts and leave their claw marks on the smooth bark of the trunks. Because the bark doesn't change in pattern as the tree grows, the scars callous over and remain visible for years. These marks should not be confused with the numerous raised "freckles" which are natural to beech bark.

Identification: Look for oval leaves with saw-toothed margins and veins that end at the tip of each tooth. Some of the stiff and leathery leaves turn light tan and remain on the twigs through the winter. The bark is light gray, resembling an elephant's skin.

Yellow (Silver) Birch

This large, tall tree has yellowish or gray bark that peels in strips; the bark is rough and scaly on older trees, and rolls back in ribbon-like curls on younger ones. The twigs smell and taste like wintergreen.

Identification: Look for long, oval, sharply double-toothed leaves that never grow opposite each other.

Eastern Hemlock

This fir is a favorite nesting tree for Golden-crowned Kinglets. It grows in dense stands in damp ravines and on north-facing slopes.

Identification: Look for short, flattened needles and tiny brown cones that hang from the tips of the tiny branchlets. The top branch in the crown usually hangs limply away from the prevailing winds.

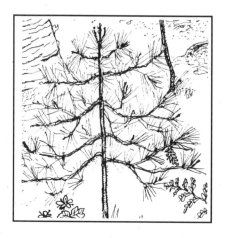

White Pine

This is the largest conifer in the northeast. It grows in openings created by logging or natural causes. Because a White Pine has difficulty reproducing in its own shade, a hardwood will likely replace it when it dies. Tall straight white pines were prized for ship masts in the colonial period. If the trees were 24 inches in diameter or thicker at the base and were within three miles of navigable water, they were called "king's pines" and were reserved for the Royal Navy. British colonists designated such trees by carving a broad arrow in the trunk.

Identification: Look for needles that bunch toward the ends of the twigs, giving the tree a clumpy appearance. The branches are spaced widely apart.

SHORT TREES AND SHRUBS (The Understory)

Beneath the canopy of tall trees is an understory of smaller ones, including Striped Maple, Gray Birch, and Pin Cherry, while a shrub you are sure to see is Hobblebush. Because the canopy trees have blocked most of the sunlight, the trees and plants beneath them need large leaves to capture what little sunlight filters through. The leaves are dark green because their chlorophyll cells are set close together in order to convert the minimal sunlight to energy efficiently.

Trees and plants more exposed to sunlight will have smaller leaves so that all their moisture doesn't evaporate. The leaves also will be lighter colored because the chlorophyll cells are more widely spaced. You can sometimes tell whether you are on a shady north-facing slope or a sunny south-facing slope simply by looking at the size and color of the leaves.

Striped Maple

This short tree with very large leaves is also known as "moose-wood," "whistlewood," or "goosefoot maple." Animals frequently eat its bark and twigs, especially in winter. Striped Maple is an insignificant tree except in the fall, when its yellow leaves brighten the forest.

Identification: Look for double saw-toothed leaves that are nearly as wide as they are long. The leaves of the Striped Maple have three points, while those of the Sugar Maple have many points. The limbs and trunk are finely lined with white streaks. The bark of young trees is greenish, but with age it turns reddish and the streaks become less noticeable.

Gray Birch

This small, white-trunked tree with dancing leaves is the species that Robert Frost affectionately described in his poem, "Birches." Look for low, bending clumps of Gray Birches in clearings, where they shade seedlings of larger trees. The trunks are so flexible that in winter their upper branches sometimes touch the ground when weighted down with snow and ice.

Identification: Look for small triangular, doubled-toothed leaves with very long tapering tips. The bark does not peel and is chalky white with black triangular blotches below each branch.

Pin Cherry

This short-lived small tree grows quickly on ground disturbed by fire or logging. Each tiny red fruit has a large stone and is sour-tasting. It's best used in jelly.

Identification: Look for glossy, long, narrow leaves tapering to a point, and hanging downward. The bark is shiny red, somewhat papery, and bitter tasting.

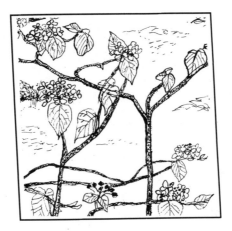

Hobblebush

This shrub with large, heart-shaped leaves is some-times the only vegetation in the understory. It spreads widely and forms dense thickets. Knowledgeable campers use hobblebush leaves as a substitute for toilet paper. Its twigs and buds are a favorite food for deer.

Identification: The flower, which blooms in May, has showy white sepals surrounding an inconspicuous flower. (In most plants, sepals are the little green cups that support the flow-ers.) Look for nearly round leaves with rusty hairs under-neath. To capture the sunlight efficiently, the leaves rarely overlap. The leaves are especially beautiful in fall, with red, orange, yellow, and purple patches interspersed with bright green veins. The berry-like fruit is tipped with a brown dot. Fruit develops red in August, but later in the fall turns black.

PLANTS

Still closer to the ground is a layer of flowers, herbs, ferns, and mosses. Lower elevations have a wider variety of plants than higher up because the weather is not as severe, fewer clouds block the sun, and the soils are sufficient to sustain more species. Plants occupy different levels, depending on the amount of light they need.

In early spring the plants closest to the ground leaf out first because there is still enough sunlight to reach them. The higher layers then leaf out from bottom to top until the trees fill in. Mosses find pockets of deep shade, while lichens search for light in the treetops.

If you visit the mountains in summer, you won't find as many flowers in bloom as you would in spring. Most completed their life cycle before the trees above them developed leaves and blocked the sun.

As a rule, mountain flowers are small and inconspicuous. To find them you will have to stop and stoop. Among the most common flowers in the Northern Hardwood forest are: Red Trillium, Pink Lady's-Slipper, Wood Sorrel, and Goldthread.

In the mountains the seasons compress and telescope. A short (or compressed) growing season means plants have to mature and reproduce in a hurry. On the other hand, because warmer temperatures come to higher elevations later, the same species of plants that have passed their peak in the valleys may just be coming into bloom higher up. The Red Trillium, for example, blooms in April at lower elevations, while blossoms can still be found in late June near the treeline. Wood Sorrel blooms in June in the valleys, but not until August higher up the slopes.

Red Trillium

Trilliums are easy to recognize because all their parts
come in threes. This plant is also known as "Stinking
Benjamin," but its beautiful, delicate maroon or purple
flower more than makes up for its foul smell.

Pink Lady's Slipper (Moccasin-Flower)

This beautiful plant is an exception to the rule about mountain flowers, as it requires no bending over to notice. From early May to as late as mid-June, lucky hikers may come across a patch of these large, showy orchids in the Northern Hardwoods Zone, as well as in bog environments. The single inflated, dark pink flowers are veined with red and rise from a pair of broad, oval leaves. After the flowers are gone, the leaves disappear into the forest litter.

Birds

The birds you will most likely see in the Northern Hardwoods are tree-climbing species. They are easier to spot than other birds because they actively hunt for food in tree trunks, as opposed to sitting quietly on a high branch, waiting for an insect to buzz by. Look for woodpeckers, nuthatches, creepers, sapsuckers, and flickers on tree trunks. All tree-climbing birds undulate when they fly.

Because tree-climbing birds have different styles of hunting, several species can co-exist in the same space. Woodpeckers go up trees in their search for food, while nuthatches go down, finding grubs the woodpeckers miss. Not to be left out, brown creepers go around trees in a spiral, targeting morsels that both the woodpeckers and nuthatches leave behind.

Most birds have four toes: three in front and one in back. With a few exceptions, tree-climbing birds have two toes in front and two in back. This gives them better purchase on tree bark.

Woodpeckers are mostly black and white, with bills like chisels for boring and spiked tails to secure themselves on tree trunks. You can identify species by the difference in patterns of black and white, as well as by their size.

Downy Woodpecker

At the lower elevations, this bird is quite common. Look for the white back and small bill. The male has a red spot on the back of the head. Its call is a rapid whinny of descending notes.

Hairy Woodpecker

The Hairy Woodpecker is simply a larger version of the Downy, but somewhat less common. Most people find it hard to tell them apart unless they are side-by-side. Otherwise, a big bill means it's a Hairy Woodpecker. Its call sounds like a frantic rattle. Both the Downy and Hairy sometimes make a single note - only the Downy says "pick" and the Hairy says "peek"!

Pileated Woodpecker

At lower and middle elevations, you might be lucky enough to see this striking black and white crow-sized bird. Look for its flaming red crest; the male has a red stripe below the eye; the female doesn't. Because Pileated Woodpeckers are rather shy, they are more often heard than seen. The call resembles a loud kik-kik-kikkik-kik-kik. Most hikers only get to see the evidence one of these birds has left behind: a few large holes in a tree trunk.

Brown Creeper

This dusty little bird resembles a big mouse with wings. Look for creepers on shade trees. They are the only tree-climbers with curved bills. You probably won't hear a Brown Creeper's call, but if you do, it will be an insignificant, high-pitched "seee."

White-Breasted Nuthatch

While woodpeckers go up trees, nuthatches go down headfirst. Two kinds live in the mountains. The larger White-Breasted Nuthatch is more common at lower elevations. You will have identified it if you see a black, gray and white bird heading down a tree. It makes a nasal "yank-yank-yank."

Red-Breasted Nuthatch

In the higher dense spruce-fir forests, look for the Red-Breasted Nuthatch. It has a rusty breast and a white stripe through the eye. It also 'yanks,' but sounds tinnier.

Yellow-Bellied Sapsucker

In the spring and summer, look for the Yellow-Bellied Sapsucker (not to be confused with a "double-breasted seersucker"). It is the only tree-climber with a long, white wingpatch. It also has a red forehead. Probably the best way to tell a sapsucker is by its scruffy appearance. Although it looks unkempt, it drills the neatest holes in the forest. A sapsucker's call is an infrequent 'cheerrr,' slurring downward.

Flicker

This large, showy bird with a brown back and spotted front is common at lower elevations. When it flies, look for a white rump and yellow under the wings and tail. If a flicker can't find food on tree trunks, it will hop on the ground, looking for ants. Its call is a loud "wicka-wicka-wicka-wicka."

In summer, songbirds are more likely to be heard than seen, for they have already mated and don't need to be on display. At this time of year they prefer to stay out of sight, for they are going through moulting, an embarrassing process of shedding their old feathers and growing new ones. After the cacophony of songs during the spring mating season, summer brings a strange and brooding stillness in the woods, interrupted only occasionally by a solitary bird song.

Thrushes are robin-sized birds (a robin, after all, is a thrush). Look for dusky gray or brown backs and spotted breasts. Each species is slightly different in coloration: the Hermit Thrush, for example, has a reddish tail, while the Wood Thrush has a reddish head. Different species of thrushes prefer different habitats: the Veery and Wood Thrush live in hardwoods at lower elevations; the Hermit Thrush can be found slightly higher up the slopes where hardwoods and spruce-firs overlap; the Swainson's Thrush even higher in the pure Boreal Forest; while the Grey-Cheeked Thrush lives in dwarf trees.

The few songs to be heard are usually at dawn and dusk, but the music at dusk is especially resonant because it consists mostly of solos, rather than the chorus heard at dawn. Thrushes are crepuscular creatures (active at twilight) and have especially beautiful songs. Listen for the organlike notes of the Veery spiraling downward, and the flutelike ee-o-lay of the Wood Thrush. The Hermit Thrush sings three or four phrases at different pitches, each preceded by a long introductory note.

Some bird songs can be heard any time of day. The White-throated Sparrow emits several plaintive whistles that carry far through the woods at all elevations. Yankee woodsmen call him "Old Sam Peabody," as his tremulous song seems to suggest; others think the song more closely resembles, "Oh, sweet Canada, Canada, Canada."

You might hear a Red-Eyed Vireo monotonously asking, "Where am I?" and answering, "Here I am" over and over again. At any time of day you can expect to hear the harsh scolding of a Blue Jay or the unmistakable "chick-a-dee-dee-dee" of the Black-capped Chickadee.

ANIMALS

The most common animals in New England's mountains are White-footed Mice and Meadow Voles, but they are rarely seen, for they spend most of their time under the litter of groundcover. Both are most active at night, so when they do come into view it's too dark to see them. Your best chance of seeing a mouse or vole in daylight is when it's dead. Screech Owls have a nasty habit of decapitating them and hanging their bodies on tree limbs.

If you are especially lucky, you might come across a Moose at twilight. These massive animals are rarely seen along the trails, preferring the roadside, where they are attracted by road salt. When you are driving, especially at dawn and dusk, be on the lookout for Moose in the highway. They are hard to see because their legs are long and spindly, and their eyes are higher than most headlight beams, so you might not see any reflection.

The animal you will most likely see in the mountains is the diminutive Red Squirrel, especially in coniferous forests, as it loves the seeds hidden in spruce cones. You may be startled when this squirrel squeals its high, scolding chatter, a sound frequently mistaken for a bird. It is actually announcing that you are on its territory. The larger Gray Squirrel, common in southern New England, is quite rare in the mountains because it feeds almost exclusively on acorns, and oak trees are not to be found among these hardwoods.

INSECTS

In a perfect world, there would be no such thing as a Black Fly. This humpbacked little pest (only one-sixteenth to one-eighth inch long) is the bane of existence to birds and mammals, including humans. The females are thirsty bloodsuckers, buzzing their way into ears, nostrils, and behind eyeglasses before you have a chance to swat them. Black Fly cocoons cover rocks of fast-flowing mountain streams. In late spring and early summer full-grown adults burst out of these cocoons, rising on a bubble of air, and fly away to inflict their misery. Some species carry wildfowl malaria, accounting for up to half the deaths of ducks, geese, swans, and turkeys. Fortunately, in the mountains of New England Black Flies are gone by the Fourth of July.

Black flies are commonly believed to be food for trout, but trout have no appetite for them. On the other hand, birds do eat black flies, perhaps out of self-defense. While only four or five species of these nasty critters bite humans, 25 species are pests to birds.

Fishermen take note: certain Black Fly repellents, such as DEET, can destroy plastic fishing lines.

Chapter 3
Nature in the Higher Elevations:
The Spruce-Fir Zone

At about 3,000 feet, the scenery will change rather abruptly as you climb into the Spruce-Fir Zone, known scientifically as the Boreal ("northern") Forest Zone. Adapting to temperatures as low as 40 degrees below zero in winter, coniferous trees, especially spruce and fir, will gradually replace the less cold-resistant hardwoods of the lower elevations. An occasional sun-loving Mountain Ash or Paper Birch can be seen growing in windfalls, where shallow-rooted conifers have blown over, allowing sunlight to penetrate.

The forests you see today began about 10,000 years ago, after the last glacier carried most of northern New England's topsoil out to sea. At first, the landscape looked the way northern Canada's arctic tundra does today. There were no trees at all - only a few hardy mosses, lichens, grasses, and shrubs could survive in the pulverized rock left under the melting ice.

Over thousands of years the mosses and lichens broke down the rocks, creating soils in which spruce and fir trees could set roots. Eventually, these hardy species adapted to the colder weather at higher elevations, climbing the mountainsides and forcing the tundra to retreat to a few wind-swept summits, where it can still be seen today.

To be able to grow in the shallow, rocky soils and harsh climate at the higher elevations, coniferous trees share certain features. For one thing, they keep their

needles (which are a form of leaf) through the winter.
Because these needles are woody and have a waxy coating, they are waterproofed from the
snow and insulated from the cold.
Also, the needles can stop growing in
winter and still survive because they
are filled with a sweet chemical that
nourishes them. (As you walk
through a spruce-fir forest, you can
smell this "anti-freeze.")

Native Americans used many species of trees to make canoes. They stripped the bark of the Paper Birch and stretched it over White Cedar frames, sewing it together with thread from Tamarack roots, then caulking the seams with White Pine or Balsam resin.

In early spring as soon as the
ground thaws, the sap in a coniferous
tree starts to run, sending fresh nutrients from the soil to its needles. This
process wakes up the tree and allows it to resume growing in a short season, giving it a headstart over trees that
lose their leaves and must sprout new ones every spring
to continue growing.

Because conifers store food in their needles, they can
live on the shallow, rocky soils of the upper elevations.
But this means that the roots are close to the surface and
don't have much of a grip. When the wind blows, you can
sometimes feel the ground move as roots of trees clinging
to the rocks are wrenched about. With little purchase,
coniferous trees can topple at random with a strong gust
or even a heavy load of snow. The chaotic debris of fallen
trees in the spruce-fir forest makes it almost impossible
for hikers to venture off the trail.

Of all the trees in the forest, coniferous trees are the
most primitive. While deciduous trees have compart-
ments, like fruits, nuts, and berries, to protect their seeds,

coniferous trees expose their seeds in open cones.

Spruce-fir forests are even darker than hardwood forests, for they develop dense canopies of needle-leaves to strain water from low-hanging clouds. Even when there is no rain, the forest is constantly dripping, especially on slopes facing away from the sun.

Prominent in spruce-fir forests are mysterious growths, called lichens (pronounced, "LIKENS"). These are not really plants, for they have no stems, leaves, or roots. Lichens can stand extreme heat, as well as extreme cold. The only thing they cannot tolerate is industrial pollution.

Some lichens attach themselves to tree trunks, where there is more sunlight than can be found on the forest floor. Others, like Old Man's Beard, grow on the inner branches of spruces and firs, hanging like Spanish Moss. Rock Tripes are papery lichens that attach themselves to rocks; in forests they thrive on water dripping from the trees, while in open spots, especially bald summits, they simply comb moisture from low clouds. During dry weather Rock Tripes become brittle and resemble burned potato chips. After a few days of rain or fog, this variety of lichen expands and becomes soft and green once more.

You can tell how much snow normally falls in an area by looking at the trunks of spruce and fir trees. They are usually dark at the base, up to the point where lichens have attached themselves to the bark, for lichens need light year-round, and rarely grow below the average snow depth. At 4,000 feet, tree trunks are usually free of lichens up to three to four feet.

TALL TREES (CANOPY)

The most common tall trees of the boreal forest are Balsam Fir and Red Spruce. As you climb higher, Red Spruces will become fewer and Balsam Firs will take over almost completely. Black Spruces can be found mixed in with Balsams near the treeline, as well as in cool valleys.

Three easy ways to tell firs and spruces apart:

- spruce cones point down, fir cones point up
- fir needles are flat, spruce needles are triangular
- to the touch, firs are "friendly," spruces are "spiney."

Balsam Fir

This symmetrical evergreen with a narrow, pointed spire is the most fragrant tree in the forest, and therefore a favorite at Christmas. Its cones don't fall from the tree; instead, the seeds dislodge, leaving small pedestals pointing upward on the branches. Scientists use a chemical from the bark to mount microscopic specimens; optometrists use the same chemical for optical cement.

Identification: At a distance, you can recognize this tree by its symmetrical shape and pointed top. Up close, look for cones growing upright, and flat needles with two silvery-white lines on the undersides.

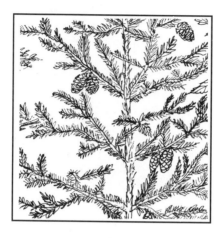

Red Spruce

This handsome tree is less pointed than the Balsam Fir. Gum from the sap in spruce tree trunks was used for chewing before chicle, a gum from a tropical tree, became popular. Spruce beer, prepared by boiling young twigs with sugar and flavorings, was a favorite soft drink from the 16th century to the early 20th.

Identification: Look for shiny, dark, olive-green needles with a yellowish tinge; the prickly, short needles point out in all directions. Shiny, reddish-brown cones hang downward and fall off the tree when they are ripe. The twigs are also reddish-brown and very hairy.

Black Spruce

This sharp-pointed evergreen of the highest elevations sometimes has a circle of babies surrounding its
drooping branches. It sprouts new trees by sending out
shoots from its lowest branches when heavy snows bend
them to the ground. The Black Spruce defends itself
against fire by clustering its cones at the top.

*Identification: Look for very short, pale blue-green needles
with a whitish tinge and sharp points. Unlike the larger
cones of the Red Spruce which fall off the tree when ripe, the
small, egg-shaped cones of the Black Spruce remain on the
tree year-round.*

SHORT TREES AND SHRUBS

The few understory trees and shrubs to be found in the spruce-fir forest will be growing in sunny gaps where Spruces and Balsams have fallen. Among the most common are: Mountain Ash, Paper Birch, Rhodora, Mountain Shadbush, Mountain Alder, and Elderberry.

Mountain Ash

Unlike the common orange-berried ornamental of New England yards, the wild variety in the mountains has large clusters of bright, coral berries. The fruit, which appears in July and stays on the tree until winter, is a favorite of many birds, especially Cedar Waxwings. Birds have been known to get drunk from fermented berries, flying into each other and even hanging upside down from branches.

Identification: Look for 13-15 tapered, sharply double-toothed leaflets on each stem. The bitter-tasting berries, crowded in five-inch clusters, ripen in late August and early September. The bark has rough, horizontal protruding scars.

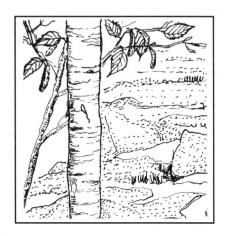

Paper (or White) Birch

This magnificent large tree with peeling white bark
has many uses. Native Americans used the bark to make
canoes. In recent times, the wood has been used to make
toothpicks, ice cream sticks, bobbins, spools, clothespins,
broom handles, and toys. The sap can be boiled down to
make syrup. The peeling bark is very tempting to remove
as a souvenir. But please remove it only from fallen logs,
as stripping it from a living tree will leave black, ugly
scars.

*Identification: Look for egg-shaped, short-pointed leaves
with double teeth. The bark on young trees is dark red and
doesn't peel.*

Rhodora.

This beautiful, small shrub grows best in rocky areas with plenty of sunshine. Its rose-purple flowers come out before the leaves do and form masses of color in mid-June. While the leaves are harmful for livestock to eat, they have no effect on deer.

Identification: Look for a shrub with straight, upright branches and oval leaves somewhat rolled along the edges.

Mountain Shadbush (Sugarplum)

This shrub with dull, green leaves grows in clusters in wet places and on slopes at the higher elevations. It stands out because of its roundness. The fruit, which ripens in July and August, is used for pies. Mountain Shadbush gets its name from blossoming at lower elevations in early May, when shad traditionally start their run upstream to spawn. At these higher elevations it blossoms in June.

Identification: Look for smooth, thin, elliptical leaves whose tip and base are about the same size. The fruit is pear-shaped and turns purple when ripe.

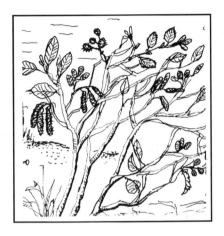

Mountain Alder

This large, pioneering shrub has many trunks growing from the same spot. It prefers wet, spongy areas, and,
like the black spruce, sometimes regenerates itself by
sending roots to the ground from low branches.

*Identification: The easiest way to identify this shrub is to
look for its fragrant catkins hanging like long tassels in the
wind. At the tips of the branches are small clusters of dark
brown fruit that resemble tiny pine cones. The finely-
toothed leaves are sometimes ruffled along the edges and
green underneath with rusty veins. The roots form dense
mats on the ground.*

Red-Berried Elder

This large shrub has foul-smelling twigs when bruised. Its small, purple berries ripen in mid- to late-summer and are sometimes so numerous they weigh down the branches. Unlike the Common Elder with its black-purple berries, the fruit of the Red-Berried Elder is not edible. Native Americans used the pithy stems for tapping the sap from maple trees, while toymakers have used them for making whistles and popguns. Wasps often build nests in the stems.

Identification: Look for saw-toothed oval leaves with sharp points on a few stout, spreading branches. The yellowish-white flowers bloom in early spring. The fruit grow in elongated clusters; not all the berries ripen, but the ones that do turn red.

PLANTS

Some plants found in the lower elevations, like Wood Sorrel and Goldthread, can eke out a living in the even cooler, darker spruce-fir forest, as well. Others to look for are Bunchberry, Yellow Clintonia, as well as Spinulose Wood Fern.

Bunchberry

If you see six leaves at the base of the plant, you will also find a cluster of insignificant greenish flowers surrounded by four large sepals that look like petals. If you see only four leaves, there will be no flowers. In either case, the sepals give this member of the dogwood family a showy appearance as late as July in the upper elevations. Later in the summer, look for a tight grouping of bright red berries.

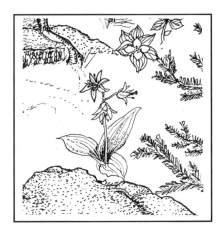

Yellow Clintonia (Blue Bead Lily)

Even in August you might find see three to six drooping, bell-like, yellow-green flowers coming from this
plant's single stem. At the base is a pair of shiny, dark
green, oblong leaves. Its fruit consists of a cluster of
exceptionally pure-blue berries, which can be slightly
poisonous.

Spinulose Woodfern

This lacy, large fern may reach three feet long and a foot wide, and grows in clusters. It is one of the few ferns to adapt to the cooler upper elevations. Florists sometimes use this delicate variety as greenery.

BIRDS

The number and variety of birds dwindle the higher up you climb. While lower elevation birds, like the Black-capped Chickadee, Red-breasted Nuthatch, and White-throated Sparrow, can be seen in the spruce-fir forest, others live in these woods exclusively: Gray-Cheeked Thrush, Winter Wren, Boreal Chickadee, and Red Crossbill.

Gray-Cheeked Thrush

This species has a dull, olive-gray back and a lightly spotted breast. With its thin, nasal song spiraling downward, then rising abruptly at the end, the Gray-Cheeked is hardly the most melodious of thrushes.

Winter Wren

Despite its name, this dark brown bird with a tiny upturned tail is a summer visitor here. Among the smallest North American songbirds, it looks more like a mouse than a bird, as it hops and darts among the tree trunks. The Winter Wren is known locally as "The Little Bird with the Big Mouth," singing an energetic and sometimes incessant series of warbles, often ending with a very high, light trill.

Boreal Chickadee

Another bird only to be found in coniferous mountain forests is a chickadee - not the familiar black-capped one seen at feeders throughout the Northeast - but the Boreal Chickadee. It looks like its cousin, but has a brown cap, back and sides. This tame little bird hops and flits high up in fir trees, extracting seeds from cones. Its song is similar to the more common black-capped but is less energetic - it drawls, "Chick-chee-day-day."

Red Crossbill

This brick-red bird is uniquely adapted to spruce-fir forests. Its bill is custom-made for extracting seeds from cones: the upper part overlaps the lower part so that when it opens its mouth, it spreads apart the cone scales and extracts the seeds with its tongue. The Crossbill moves about the trees like a parrot, using both its bill and its feet for leverage. It is not afraid of humans, and you might be able to get quite close to one. Crossbills are attracted to road salt and are frequently killed by traffic in winter.

Chapter 4
The Landscape in Miniature: The Alpine Tundra Zone

Above treeline is an environment completely different from any in New England: the Alpine Tundra Zone. This region has a lot going against it. Plants have to survive in poor, shallow soils, a growing season of less than three months, foggy weather, extremely cold temperatures, and high winds. Despite all this, you will find a community of hardy plants and grasses that survive here. The fact that anything can grow under these harsh conditions serves as a reminder that what may seem like a hostile environment to humans is not necessarily hostile to other forms of life.

At the summit of Mount Washington:
- *The highest temperature ever recorded is 72 degrees.*
- *The highest wind speed on earth (231 mph) was recorded here*
- *The average wind speed (35 mph) is four times that of the lowlands.*
- *Hurricane winds (over 70 mph) are recorded every month.*
- *In the winter of 1957-58, 344 inches of snow fell.*
- *Clouds block the sun 75 percent of the time.*

Unlike the vast, desolate stretches of tundra in northern Canada, New England tundra is limited to peaks over 4,000 feet, and a few rocky shoulders at lower elevations. The largest area is in the Presidential Range of the White Mountains, about seven and one-half square miles extending from Mount Madison in the north to Mount Pleasant in the south, with Mount Washington in the

middle. In Vermont's Green Mountains, tundra consists of only 250 acres on Mount Mansfield and Camel's Hump; while in Maine, tundra can be found on Mount Katahdin, Saddleback Mountain, Bigelow Mountain, and some of the higher peaks of the Mahoosuc Range.

The boundary between this alpine tundra and the spruce-fir forest below it is well defined, with few of the same species living on both sides. You will see no upright trees in the tundra, only a few birds, and no animals.

As you explore these rocky summits up close, it will become clear that they are not as bald as they seemed from a distance. Growing things can be found everywhere on these windy peaks, but in most cases you will have to get down on your hands and knees to identify them.

On almost every rock you will find lichens. These unusual growths produce acids that over thousands of years form cracks in the rocks, eventually creating enough soil for pioneering plants to take root. The species you will likely notice first are Map Lichens, forming large yellow patches that look like islands and continents on the rocks. Other rocks will be covered with crusty gray-green circles of Ring Lichens.

In areas where soil has covered the bedrock, the alpine zone is carpeted with sedges. These grass-like plants have thick, triangular stems ("sedges have edges") and narrow-bladed leaves - adaptations to prevent water from evaporating. By contrast, grasses have round stems.

Sedges form lush meadows on the coldest slopes, where the clouds touch the ground, providing plenty of moisture. Individual plants of Highland Sedge can be identified by two or three thin leaves pointing upward,

surrounding small spikes on a stiff stem up to two feet
tall; these leaves turn brown early in the summer.
Another common sedge is Alpine (or Bigelow's) Sedge.
This plant is about a foot tall, with most of the leaves
hugging the base of the stem.

TREES

At the bottom edge of the alpine tundra zone, you will notice that the spruces and firs look much different than those seen growing lower down the trail. These trees, mostly Black Spruce, have become so stunted that some even grow flat on their sides, forming mats along the ground. Many have limbs on only one side - away from the wind; these are called "flag trees."

This area of dwarf, misshapen trees is called *krummholz*, a German word meaning "twisted wood." The trees grow close to the ground for protection from the strong winds and heavy snows. You won't find any cones on the spruces in the *krummholz:* in such a short growing season, these trees reproduce by sending shoots into the ground rather than by the slower process of growing cones with seeds in them.

SHRUBS and PLANTS

In open areas and in crevices between the rocks you will find a variety of miniature plants and shrubs - each efficiently adapted to deal with small variations in terrain and the harsh climate above treeline. Because most of these plants and shrubs are evergreens, they don't need to grow new leaves every year. They also have tiny leaves and flowers, so that there is less plant to nurture and also fewer surfaces exposed to the wind. Heaths, like blueberries and cranberries, are shrubs with tough, woody stems and leathery leaves to conserve moisture. Many alpine plants grow in dense mats to create warmth, as well as to screen moisture from low-hanging clouds.

While all alpine plants grow from roots and bulbs, some do produce seeds - hundreds of them. But the seeds rarely travel more than a few feet, for while the wind may be strong to humans, at the level where these ground-hugging plants live, it drops off significantly. Of the plants that actually do grow from seed, almost none survive a second season.

Because the growing season here is so short, tundra plants cannot afford the luxury that annuals have of starting from seed every year, growing into adult plants, flowering, and producing a few more seeds to create new plants the next season. Instead, all species of plants in the alpine tundra zone are perennials, growing from roots and bulbs underground. In fact, the tiny plants you see on the surface are but the tip of the iceberg: there may be as much as ten times their mass underground.

Please note: Please be careful where you walk; it takes years for a plant to mature here, but only a second for a careless hiker to destroy it. While plants in the alpine tundra zone can withstand just about any amount of nasty weather, their brittle leaves are vulnerable to hikers' boots. Also the thin soils are easily compacted by footsteps.

Mountain Cranberry

Look for this low shrub (only six inches high) among the grasses on more protected south- and east-facing slopes. The shiny, evergreen leaves are as thick as plastic. This cranberry has pink, bell-shaped flowers. The dark, red berries, which appear in late summer, are only good cooked as sauce.

Alpine Azalea

This is another small evergreen with pink flowers. But, unlike Mountain Cranberry, this plant grows in mats and lives on the most windswept, north- and west-facing exposures. The flowers form masses of color in early June.

Lapland Rosebay

This foot-high evergreen shrub also forms mats on wind-swept exposures. The showy purple flowers, which bloom from late May to mid-June, are about an inch wide.

Alpine (Dwarf) Bilberry

Look for this six-inch tall shrub in protected areas. It looks like a Blueberry with toothed leaves. Picking the berries is a tedious process, as you have to get down on your hands and knees. The largest cluster will consist of three berries, more likely only one or two.

Black Crowberry

This trailing shrub forms mats along the ground in
the same regions as the Alpine Bilberry. Many of its small,
needle-like leaves face downward. The black berries,
which appear in July and August, are not very tasty, and
best left for the birds.

Diapensia

On slopes exposed to the worst weather this may be
the only flowering plant you will see, for it is one of few
species that can survive the winter without a protective
blanket of snow. Diapensia grows in compact cushions
that create their own warmth; the leathery leaves are
tightly packed for protection against the wind. While this
plant blossoms in June, it forms buds the previous year;
the buds stay ice-covered through the winter, waiting for
a sunny day in June to blossom.

*Identification: The tiny flowers on short upright stems have
five bright, white petals. Though some flowers last into July,
you are more likely to see just the green seed pods held erect
over a cushion of waxy leaves.*

Mountain Sandwort

This plant's delicate white flowers grow so densely as to resemble snowballs. Hikers have been known to use sandwort tufts as trail markers on moonlit nights. The wire-thin leaves are interwoven to trap what little warmth there is at ground level. This is one of the few alpine plants to bloom throughout the summer.

Identification: Look for tiny, five-petaled white flowers on thin stems with narrow leaves.

BIRDS

The species of birds found here can be counted on one hand, for there is only a limited supply of food and the weather is inhospitable. Unlike almost all the plants in the alpine tundra zone, none of the birds seen here is endemic, or live only in this kind of habitat.

Many species of birds spend only the summer here. Like many songbirds, the Blackpoll Warbler becomes a true long-distance flyer in the fall, migrating as far south as the tropical rain forests of Brazil to spend the winter. The following spring it returns to the frigid mountaintops of New England to breed. Migrating species can survive only as long as the habitats at both ends of their range - and the restings spots in between - remain hospitable to them. For these birds, environmental preservation is truly a global issue.

Raven

Above the treeline, you might see a glossy black bird that looks like a very large crow. But unlike its gregarious cousin, the Raven is shy and wary. This strong and graceful flier can hold its position motionless even in the strongest gales. The Raven's most prominent field marks are a heavy arched bill, curved like a "Roman nose," and a ruffle of beard-like feathers around the throat. Its call is a hoarse "croak-croak," usually when in flight.

Slate-colored Junco

Along any trail, especially near the treeline, you are almost guaranteed to spot this chunky little gray bird with white outer tail feathers. In fact, in any season you will likely see lots of juncos hopping along the ground and flitting among the krummholz. Its call is a light twitter.

White Mountain Butterfly

Only on the highest bald peaks and only on sunny days in July are you likely to see this unusual insect. Most people associate butterflies with warm environments, but this species has adapted to the harshest climate imaginable. It may be the oldest living creature in New England, having followed the melting ice sheets northward 10,000 years ago.

It is almost impossible to see one of these creatures unless it is flying, for its protective gray-mottled coloring blends perfectly with lichen-covered rocks. Instead of fluttering like most butterflies, the White Mountain Butterfly simply lifts up a few inches from one rock and settles down on the next one. When it is not in the air, this butterfly often lies on its side, with its wing tips pointing away from the wind.

Chapter 5
The Self-Contained Landscape: Bogs

If tundra isn't other-worldly enough for you, try visiting a bog. Bogs are remnants of the Ice Age, pockets of cold created when the last retreating glacier left large chunks of ice behind. As the chunks melted, glacial debris trapped beneath them would sink, forming a kettle pond. With no streams flowing into or out of the pond, the water became stagnant - a perfect place for highly adaptive plants to colonize.

Bog water is so cold and acidic that decomposition of organisms can take centuries. In Europe, bodies of executed prisoners have been found in bogs - preserved in almost perfect condition after thousands of years.

Here in New England, most bogs develop in kettle ponds at lower elevations. Alpine bogs, by contrast, are formed by rain and melted snow collecting in depressions in bedrock along ridge tops. These are especially numerous in the Mahoosucs, along the Maine-New Hampshire border.

A pond becomes a bog when colonizing plants spread across it and fill it in, creating a mat of spongy ground thick enough to walk on. The first plants to invade are thick-leaved shrubs, called Leatherleaf. As branches hanging over the water become heavy with foliage, they droop below the surface. New shoots develop under water, forming a dense tangle - suitable for Sphagnum Moss to take root.

Sphagnum Moss has been called the "keeper of the bog." With its ability to absorb tremendous amounts of

water, it quickly spreads across the entire pond, creating a floating mat for other plants to take up residence. Over time, the mat thickens, preventing the water in the pond from circulating or the sun from warming the layers below.

Sphagnum Moss creates an acid that prevents dead organic matter from decomposing. When a bog plant

Methane gas is a major player in the global warming process that threatens our atmosphere. Besides bogs, other major sources of methane are rice paddies, landfill wastes, brush fires, and sheep and cattle.

dies, its remains simply sink to the bottom and stay there, steeping and turning the water the color of strong tea. Gradually the thickening mat above and the accumulating plant debris at the bottom meet, forming a giant sponge as much as 40 feet thick. In this environment all growth slows down, for the water is cold, and the few nutrients that can exist in the acid don't circulate.

Hikers may have trouble getting through the thick tangle of undergrowth in a bog. Walking on the spongy mat is like walking on a giant waterbed, and it's easy to sink down. As you venture into a bog you might release gas bubbles from decaying plants. These bubbles contain methane - pure natural gas - and can be ignited, producing a blue flame with a "poof."

From the air a bog look like a giant bull's-eye, with tall tamaracks and spruces on the outer circles, and shorter tamaracks closer in. Nearer the center is a dense ring of shrubs and grasses living on a mat of sphagnum moss, while the bull's-eye itself may still have open water in it.

TREES

Few species of trees have been able to adapt to the bog environment. Tamarack, by far, is the most common. In old filled bogs you might come across Black Spruce, Balsam Fir, or Paper Birch (all described in Chapter 3).

Tamarack (American Larch)

This slow-growing species is unusual because it is a deciduous tree with needles and cones, giving it the appearance of a conifer. Unlike coniferous needles which stay green and last through the winter, the Tamarack's turn bright yellow and drop in the fall, creating what looks like a dead fir tree. In spring, fresh needles create a beautiful light green gauze on the branches.

A Tamarack living in a nutrient-poor bog grows much more slowly than one living on dry land: a 100-year-old bog tree might be only ten feet tall and have a trunk only three inches thick, while a tree the same age living in better soils might be more than 40 feet tall with a 12-inch trunk.

Identification: Look for a coniferous-looking tree with a pointed top and widely spaced, feathery branches. It may be the only tree in a bog, and certainly the only one with yellow needles in the fall.

SHRUBS

Bog shrubs consist of only a few species. Most are evergreen heath plants adapted to conserve moisture with tough, woody stems and stiff, leathery leaves.

Labrador Tea

To capture water in the atmosphere, this shrub's leaves are coated with rusty fur and are rolled inward at the edges to keep the liquid from escaping. The leaves are fragrant when crushed and make a bad imitation of tea when steeped. In June, look for clusters of small, white flowers. The long, narrow leaves turn orange in fall, some lasting through the winter.

Leatherleaf

This low shrub has many branches. As the name suggests, the tough, leathery leaves are covered with small, rough scales. In spring, look for small, white flowers hanging in a line under the stem.

Bog Rosemary (Andromeda)

This evergreen has long, narrow leaves with sharp tips. The leaves are pale blue-green on top, whitish underneath, and have edges that curl inward. The clusters of small, white, bell-shaped flowers bloom in May.

Pale (Bog) Laurel

This shrub, like Bog Rosemary, has leaves that are whitish underneath and rolled in at the edges, but they are broader, shorter, and have blunt tips. The showy clusters of pink flowers bloom in May and June.

PLANTS

Because their roots may be frozen as late as July and there are few nutrients in the water anyway, plants on the surface of the sphagnum mats use their leaves to collect what they need from the atmosphere, including rain, dust, and even insects.

Sphagnum Moss

This is the plant that forms the spongy mat for other plants to live on. It is the color of brown leather and has tiny, clustered leaves, giving it a manicured appearance. Because it can absorb a great amount of liquid, Native Americans used Sphagnum Moss for diapers. It is used commercially for shipping live plants.

Pitcher Plant

This striking carniverous plant has large, reddish-green leaves that form cups to hold rainwater. The lips are colorful and fragrant to attract insects. An insect landing on the lip will usually follow the leaf's red veins down the slippery inner surface, lose its grip, and slide into a deadly cocktail of rainwater and enzymes waiting at the bottom. The plant's enzymes liquefy the insect, making it digestible.

Sticky, downward-facing hairs ensure that the Pitcher Plant's prey won't escape. To make matters worse, spiders often weave their webs across the lips of the leaves, so if a captured insect doesn't drown inside the plant, it will probably be caught at the top by a spider. Blooming at low elevations from June to August, a single purplish-red flower nods on top of a foot-long stem.

Sundew

Another carnivorous plant, the Sundew is smaller than the Pitcher Plant and harder to spot in the sphagnum mat. Its reddish leaves lie flat in a circle beneath a single stem and are tipped with sticky spines that work like flypaper. When an insect lands on a leaf, the spines trap it and the leaf folds around it. Once a captured insect has been digested, the leaf unfolds and is ready for the next victim. Sundews grow to a height of only three inches. The small, white flowers grow in a row on one side of a curved stem and are in bloom from June to August.

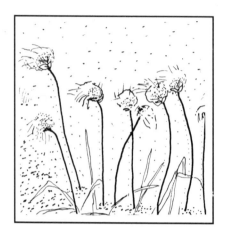

Hare's Tale (Cottongrass)

Along the edges of bogs this tall, leafless sedge is hard to miss. At the top of each spike is a tuft of white hairs.

APPENDIX

RECOMMENDED TRAILS

All times and distances are round-trip. Consult the AMC trail guides for detailed descriptions of New Hampshire and Maine trails, and the Green Mountain Club's *Guide Book of the Long Trail*, and *Day Hiker's Guide to Vermont* for trails in that state.

The following trails in New Hampshire and Maine are listed from west to east:

1. **Lonesome Lake Trail**, Franconia Notch, NH. Easy. 2 mi., 2 hr. (additional 0.8 mi., 25 min. if you take the Around-Lonesome-Lake Trail loop). The trail begins at the Lafayette Place parking lot on the west side of I-93 and climbs through Northern Hardwoods to the lake. The hike around the lake, using portions of other trails, passes through bogs on the west side.

2. **Pondicherry Wildlife Refuge**, Whitefield, NH. Easy. 2 mi., 1 hr. Access is from the east side of the Whitefield Airport. Drive or walk along the abandoned railroad line to the end of the runway; turn right and walk along active railroad tracks for about 0.75 mi. to Waumbek junction; turn left, cross the bridge, and in about 100 yds. you will come to a clearing where there is a fine view of Big Cherry Pond. Along the way you will pass bands of open bogs and swamp forest. The refuge is owned by the Audubon Society of New Hampshire.

3. **Series of Trails Forming Loop**, Crawford Notch, NH. Moderate. 7.7 mi., 7 hr. Start at the **Crawford Path**, opposite the Crawford House site on Rte. 302, just south of the parking area. After a moderate but steady climb up the east side of Crawford Notch, at 1.7 mi. turn right on the **Mizpah Cutoff**; at 0.6 mi. turn right on the **Webster Cliff Trail** (or turn left and hike 0.1 mi. to the Mizpah Spring Hut, a good place to seek shelter or enjoy a picnic lunch); follow the **Webster Cliff Trail** south for 3 mi. to the **Webster-Jackson Trail**; turn right (north) and return to Rte. 302, opposite the AMC Information Center, 0.25 mi. south of the trailhead where you started. This series of trails passes through Northern Hardwoods, the Spruce-Fir Zone, an Alpine Bog, and a small area of Alpine Tundra.

4. **Nancy Pond Trail**, Crawford Notch, NH. Moderate. 7 mi., 5 hr. 40 min. (roundtrip to Nancy Pond). This trail begins on the west side of US Rte. 302, 2.8 mi. north of the Sawyer Rock picnic area. Look for waterfalls, a pond, bogs, and a fine, moss-carpeted stand of spruces that have never been logged. If you're up to it, you can continue another 4.6 mi (2 hr. 20. min) to Desolation Shelter, via Carrigain Notch Trail, passing Little Norcross and Norcross Ponds along the way.

5. **Edmands Path**, Crawford Notch, NH. Moderate. 6.2 mi. 5 hr. 30 min. This well-designed trail to the top of Mt. Eisenhower begins on the east side of Mt. Clinton Rd., 2.3 mi. north of the Crawford House site. Passing

through Northern Hardwoods and Spruce-Firs, it provides the quickest and easiest access to a true Alpine Tundra Zone. **Take note:** The last 0.2 mi. is open and exposed to strong northwest winds.

6. **Imp Trail,** Pinkham Notch, Gorham, NH. Moderate. 6 mi., 4 hr. 10 min. Start from Rte. 16 one mile south of the Dolly Copp Campground. Follow the signs all the way, returning to Rte. 16, 0.3 mi. south of the trailhead. This loop hike offers fine views of the Presidential Range from a cliff which bears the Imp profile, as well as a chance to view a small community of alpine plants.

7. **Old Jackson Rd.,** Pinkham Notch, Gorham, NH. Easy-Moderate. 3.6 mi., 2 hr. 30 min. This trail starts from the Tuckerman Ravine Trail, about 50 yd. from the Pinkham Notch Camp, and continues to the Mt. Washington Auto Rd. You will hike through Northern Hardwoods and Spruce-Firs to a rocky outcropping with alpine plants and great views.

8. **Church Pond Loop Trail,** Albany, NH. Easy. 2.4 mi., 1 hr. 15 min. Access from Kancamagus Highway at the west end of the Passaconaway Campground (near site #18). This short hike requires little climbing, but be prepared to wade across two streams. After crossing the streams, turn left at the junction in the woods. The trail crosses two open bogs before emerging on a knoll overlooking Church Pond. Continue straight to loop back to the junction in the woods.

9. **Baldface Circle Trail**, Evans Notch, NH. Moderate. 9.6 mi., 6 hr. 30 min. This loop trail near the New Hampshire-Maine border leaves NH Rte. 113 about .2 mi. north of the entrance to the AMC Cold River Camp. Follow the trail 0.7 mi. to Circle Junction, where the loop begins. You can go in either direction to appreciate this trail, as it traverses 4.0 mi. of open ledge with unobstructed views. You will pass through Northern Hardwoods and a small Spruce-Fir forest to a bald-faced ridge with some alpine vegetation. Look for low, sweet blueberries along the ridge.

10. **Old Speck** and **Mahoosuc Trails**, Grafton Notch, ME. Moderate-Difficult. 7.8 mi., 6 hr. 50 min. This trail begins at the north side of a parking lot on ME Rte. 26, about 2.7 mi. northwest of Screw Auger Falls. Follow the trail 3.5 mi. to the Mahoosuc Trail and continue another 3.9 mi. to Old Speck Summit. You will pass through Northern Hardwoods and a fine Spruce-Fir forest to an observation tower at the top. Old Speck Trail is part of the Appalachian Trail and is blazed in white.

11. **Bigelow Range Trail**, Stratton, ME. Moderate. 6.4 mi., 5 hr. 20 min. This trail starts on ME Rtes. 27/16, 0.5 mi. southeast of Stratton. Park along the dirt road east of Rtes. 27/16. The trail begins on a logging road 0.8 mi. from the highway, passing through Northern Hardwoods, Spruce-Fir, and Alpine Zones on the way to Cranberry Peak. Along the ridge, you will traverse several open ledges with excellent views.

12. **Helon N. Taylor Trail**, Mount Katahdin, ME. Moderate-Difficult 6.2 mi., 5 hr. 35 min. (as far as Pamola Summit). This rocky trail up the north side of Mount Katahdin starts on the Chimney Pond Trail 0.1 mi. west of the Roaring Brook Campground. You will pass through a burned area, as well as a fine stand of Spruce-Firs, on the way to an Alpine Zone at Pamola Summit. Look for felsenmeer (a boulder field) near the top. While you can continue past Pamola Summit along the Knife Edge to Baxter Peak, this very narrow section of the trail goes along a serrated ridgetop and is for experienced climbers only.

Sylvia Plumb, of the Green Mountain Club, recommends the following trails in Vermont, listed from south to north (please stay off side trails, if they are posted for nesting peregrine falcons):

1. **Weathersfield Trail**, Windsor. Moderate. 6 mi., 4 hr. 30 min. This trail up the south side of Ascutney Mountain begins near a state park information board at the end of a parking lot on Cascade Falls Rd., 3.6 mi. north of its intersection with VT 131. The trail passes dramatic waterfalls and at several points offers great views of the Connecticut River Valley. At the summit, however, you will be reminded of civilization by a cluster of communications antennas and flocks of hang-gliders. (You can also reach the top by driving a paved road from VT 44A on the east side through the park entrance 4.0 mi

to a parking area 0.9 mi. below the summit. This moderate hike takes 1 hr. 15 min. round-trip.) Ascutney Mountain is a monadnock - a unique formation standing by itself where the hills around it, composed of softer material, have been worn away.

2. **White Rocks/Ice Beds Trail**, Wallingford. Easy. 1.6 mi., 1 hr. 30 min. This trail begins at the White Rocks picnic area, off Sugar Hill Rd. and 5.0 mi. south of VT 140. It affords a fine view of White Rocks Cliffs and the "Ice Beds" at the base of an old rock slide, where ice which has formed in the winter remains through the summer.

3. **Clarendon Gorge** and **Airport Lookout,** Shrewsbury. Easy. 1.4 mi., 1 hr. This section of the Long Trail begins where it crosses VT 103, just east of Rutland. Take the trail 500 ft. south to impressive Clarendon Gorge, crossing a suspension bridge over the Mill River. Turn right at the end of the bridge and climb for .7 mi. to Airport Lookout, with wonderful views to the west.

4. **Camel's Hump Loop**, Huntington. Difficult. 7.4 mi., 6 hr. The trail begins at the "Couching Lion Farm" parking lot, off Camel's Hump Rd. You will start on the **Forestry Trail** for 1.3 mi., turning left onto the **Dean Trail**. After 0.8 mi. turn right onto the **Long Trail**. (Or continue straight 0.2 mi. to reach the Montclair Glen Lodge, where bunks are available for a small fee.) Hike north on the **Long Trail** for 1.9 mi. to the summit of Camel's Hump. Continue north to reach the junction

with the **Forestry Trail** at 0.3 mi. Turn right and follow it
3.1 mi. back to the parking lot. Along this scenic loop
you will pass a beaver pond and hike through Alpine
Tundra near the summit. Please stay on the trail here.

5. **Mount Mansfield Loop**, Underhill. Difficult. 5.2
mi., 5 hr. The **Sunset Ridge Trail**, the first section of the
loop, starts 1.0 mi. beyond Underhill State Park at a sharp
turn on the old CCC road. Follow it for 3.3 mi. to the
Long Trail, where you will turn right and hike along the
ridge for 0.2 mi. to the **Canyon Trail**. Turn right and
continue 0.6 mi. to the **Halfway House Trail**. Turn right
again and hike 0.9 mi. to the CCC road, which will take
you back to the trailhead. On this hike you will pass two
bogs as well as Alpine Tundra. The **Canyon Trail** goes
through a chasm where you actually climb ladders.

6. **Devil's Gulch**, Eden. Moderate. 5 mi., 2 hr. 45 min.
This section of the **Long Trail** starts where it crosses VT
118, 5.0 mi. west of the village of Eden (VT 100). Follow
the white-blazed trail south for 1.7 mi. to Ritterbush
Lookout, continuing another 0.8 mi. to Devil's Gulch.
The gulch is a beautiful and secluded spot, filled with
ferns. Retrace your steps to return to your car.

7. **Mount Pisgah**, Westmore. Moderate. **South Trail**
round-trip to summit 3.4 mi., 2 hr. 45 min. **North Trail**
round-trip to summit 4.4 mi., 3 hr. 15 min. Loop, including scenic 3.0 mi. walk along the highway, is 6.9 mi., 4 hr.
Both trails begin at parking areas three miles apart on VT
5A along the east shore of Lake Willoughby and connect

at the top. You can take either one and retrace your steps, or both, returning to your car by walking along the scenic highway. The dramatic cliffs of Mount Pisgah and the beauty of Lake Willoughby make this one of the loveliest spots in the Northeast. Spur trails near the cliffs may be closed between May 15 and July 15 due to nesting peregrine falcons.

Checklist/Index

Notes

Notes

Notes

Notes